[handwritten signature and inscription]

Best W??

?? 2020

HIRING A CAR

and walking

AFTER IT

HIRING A CAR

and walking

AFTER IT

A little book of life lessons

Ted Corcoran

ISBN: 978-1-946195-41-8

First Printing: 2019

Cover Design and Interior Design by FuzionPress

FuzionPrint.com

DEDICATION

This book is dedicated to my maternal grandmother, Brigid Griffin. Affectionately known as Nan to my two younger siblings and I, Brigid, then aged seventy, took over the arduous task of rearing three small children, aided by my father Ned and grandfather Jack Griffin, when my mother passed away.

She did a wonderful job in a tiny cottage, deep in the countryside, with no electricity, or running water and her only means of transport a pony and trap.

Thank you Nan.

TABLE OF CONTENTS

Foreword | 9

1. Hiring a car and walking after it | 11
2. You've got to have a "WHY!" | 14
3. What will your legacy be? | 16
4. What the management regard as important, the staff pay attention to | 19
5. The main thing is to keep the main thing the main thing | 21
6. You can beat eggs, but you can't beat experience | 23
7. The way we do things around here | 25
8. Are you a monkey collector? | 27
9. The Lone Ranger Manager | 30
10. The Pareto Principle | 32
11. Is your song still unsung? | 34
12. Do or do not. There is no try | 38
13. Managing versus Doing | 40
14. A meeting is an event where minutes are kept and hours are wasted | 42
15. "Until we can manage time, we can manage nothing else" | 44
16. Paying the price | 46
17. The Eisenhower Method | 48
18. You must listen to thunder | 50
19. Don't let the little things get you! | 52
20. Are you done yet? | 54
21. If you aren't fired with enthusiasm, you will be fired, with enthusiasm | 56
22. All of it! | 59
23. There is no "I" in TEAM | 61
24. If you can read, you can learn | 64
25. The Universe always answers | 67

26. Are you a talker or a communicator? |70
27. A million to one chance, or was
    it even greater? |73
28. Measure twice, cut once |77
29. The Meitheal |80
30. Leadership is action, not position |83
31. It's not what happens to you…. |86
32. Mind the Gap |89
33. Six degrees of separation |91
34. It always seems impossible
    until it's done |94
35. Speak of the devil |97
36. Are Mission Statements ever read? |101
37. No awareness – no change |103
38. The 7 habits of highly
    successful leaders |105
39. The Leadership Bus |107
40. If you don't ask, nobody will hear you |110
41. None of us is as smart as all of us |113
42. Why What How |115
43. Money won't make you happy, but
    happy people will make you money |118
44. "I have a dream" |120
45. Do you know any grasshoppers? |124
46. Walking my fields |127
47. Sometimes the force is NOT with you |130
48. Old Man River |133
49. You will be the same person
    in five years… |136
50. There had to be a chapter 50! |138
About the author |140
Acknowledgements |141

FOREWORD

Ted is an amazing leader, communicator, mentor and storyteller. His wealth of experiences shared in this book will serve as a welcome guide to support you in your leadership journey. I have admired and learned from Ted for 20 years. He believed in me before I believed in myself, and for that I am eternally grateful. I believe in Ted! You should too! Reading Ted's lessons is as powerful as if he was talking directly to you. Thank you, Ted, for your gift of these lessons. Read this book, share it with others, and transform your life!

Gary Schmidt
International President 2009-2010,
Toastmasters International

10 Ted Corcoran

Chapter One

HIRING A CAR AND WALKING AFTER IT

Are you sometimes guilty of hiring a car and walking after it? My late grandmother, Brigid Griffin, had many "sayings" unique to herself. "It's like hiring a car and walking after it," she would say. Nan, as she was known in my family, lived about 5 miles from the nearest town, Killarney, Co. Kerry. Now and again - this was back in the early '50s - she would hire a car and driver to bring her shopping there.

The wisdom behind the saying is pretty obvious. There's no point hiring a car and walking after it. Far better that you get on board and let the car carry you to your destination. An example of what Nan meant would be hiring a painter to paint your house and then insist on doing it all yourself.

Many newly promoted managers fall into the trap of continuing to "do" rather than "manage." Leaving a "doing job" for a "management position" is a difficult change for most people. The temptation is to continue doing some of the work the staff are supposed to do. The reason is simple. People are more comfortable in their previous role. Some common reasons are the following:

1. I can do it better than they can.
2. I like to remind my team that I can do everything I ask them to do.
3. We'd never get through the work load if I didn't pitch in.
4. I feel guilty when I'm not "doing" as I seem to be less busy.
5. I feel more comfortable doing, than I do managing.

The major reason, though, must be that they have received little or no management training.

Riding home on the train around 11pm one night, a man sat opposite me and began working on his laptop. As I gazed out the window, I suddenly heard him ask, "would you have a paper tissue on you?"

I looked around and saw he had a minor nose bleed. "I'm sorry," I told him, "I haven't, but if you pinch your nostrils and hold your head back, it will stop pretty quickly."

He duly did this and after a few minutes, the nosebleed had ceased and he returned to his laptop.

"Catching up on some work?" I asked. "Yes," he said. "I'm very busy right now."

"You're a manager?" I queried. "Yes," he replied. "For about a year?" I asked. "A year and a half," was his response. "Helping your staff cope?" I prompted. "I'm so busy during the day helping them," he said, "that I have to do my own work after hours and at home."

With that, the train stopped at the next station and he was gone.

I'll leave it up to you to decide had he, indeed, hired a car, but continued to walk after it?

Chapter Two

YOU'VE GOT TO HAVE A "WHY!"

Simon O. Sinek is a British/American author and motivational speaker. He is the author of four books, including his 2009 best seller: "Start With Why: How Great Leaders Inspire Everyone to Take Action." He is probably best known for his much-discussed TED Talk: "How Great Leaders Inspire Action," which is listed as the third most popular TED presentation of all time. This details what makes great leaders and how they are able to inspire people so readily.

He argues that inspiring people is a far more powerful method for influencing human behaviour than manipulating them. Great leaders have a "Why" and are able to inspire their followers with the same.

When people have a "Why" or a deep sense of purpose, they are driven to achieve their goals. In the book, Sinek tells us if we start with a "Why," then the "How" and the "What" follows. He describes this as the Golden Circle. This, of course, applies to organisations as well as to individuals.

I have a personal experience of the importance of having a "Why." Back in time, when I was a much younger man, I completed a few marathons just short of the four-hour mark. To run 26 miles and 385 yards, without being carried away on a stretcher two thirds of the way through, requires a great deal of training. As the Dublin marathon is always held at the end of October, training, for me, began early in the New Year. Month after month, the training, and the mileage covered, steadily built up. By June, I was running a ten-mile circuit at least once a week. One evening, coming close to home, having completed nine miles or so, I came to a stop at a railway level crossing where the automatic barriers had descended. Under the bright evening sun, I was standing there, breathing heavily, with sweat rolling down my face, when suddenly, out of nowhere, this thought flashed into my head. "Why am I doing this?" was the question. I stood there and no good answer came to me. I was never going to break any records. I had already run a number of marathons and I was never going to do much better than four hours, no matter how hard I trained. The thought of keeping up this level of training, for another four months suddenly became a daunting task. No longer having a "Why" I quit on the spot, jogged slowly home and never ran another marathon.

Have you a "Why" for whatever goals you set yourself?

If you have no "Why" success becomes extremely difficult, if not impossible.

Chapter Three

WHAT WILL YOUR LEGACY BE?

If the truth be known, we would all like to leave a legacy of some sort. Something not to be placed on our headstone, but some memories to be fondly held by those who knew and loved us.

These memories need not be of great achievements in sporting, political, or business circles, but every day actions that make a difference to someone. Being kind to someone who needs our help. Being a mentor to someone who needs our advice. Being a coach to someone who needs our skills. Just being friendly, full stop.

The list is endless.

These actions may seem inconsequential to you but can make a world of difference to the recipients. Sometimes, the only way you know that you've made this difference is when, even many years later, you meet that person unexpectedly and they mention the help you were to them.

The opposite is also true. During the course of your life many people may have helped you in so many ways – ways indeed you probably can't remember.

Here in Ireland, funerals are very well attended. Support for the bereaved family is tangible, demonstrated by the big numbers who turn up for the services. The deceased's legacy is being publicly honoured and acknowledged.

But, sometimes, there are exceptions.

Many years ago, when I was serving as the Station Master (station manager) at Heuston Rail Station, Ireland's largest railway station, I was standing with a staff member at the gate to one of the platforms. An elderly man passed through and ten seconds later he collapsed and died on the platform, despite our frantic efforts to save him.

The next day, I attended his removal from the funeral home at the nearby hospital. I was anxious to tell his relatives about his collapse and the efforts made to save him, knowing that, if he was my relative, I would be grateful for the information.

The removal was timed for 4 p.m., but as it got closer, I noticed there was nobody else in attendance. Thinking I had misjudged the time, I approached the undertaker and asked him was the removal at 4 p.m. "Yes," he said, "we leave then." "But," I said, "there's nobody here." To my consternation, he replied, "Yes, you are the only one."

And so, on the dot of 4 p.m., the poor man's coffin was loaded into the hearse and the undertaker drove out the gate and out of view.

I can still clearly recall the crunch the wheels made on the loose gravel as it left, as I stood alone watching, while the sun shone from a clear blue summer sky.

Who was this man? Where were his friends and family? What legacy had he left that nobody felt it worthwhile to attend his funeral?

I still don't know the answers but my fervent hope is that you and I never find ourselves alone and in a similar situation.

What will your legacy be?

Chapter Four

WHAT THE MANAGEMENT REGARD AS IMPORTANT, THE STAFF PAY ATTENTION TO

You can replace the word staff with volunteers, even children, or any group of people working in a business, organisation or group – but the principle remains the same. If management does not consistently emphasise what's important, quite soon staff will decide their own priorities. It's never enough for top management to set out what is important once and believe it travels down to the staff with the same degree of importance.

Remember the old story about the officer in command on a war frontline sending back, before radio, a message by word of mouth? The message simply said, "Send reinforcements, we're going to advance." By the time it got back to the generals holed up in HQ, it had changed to: "Send three and fourpence, we're going to a dance."

Safety was the number one priority in my organisation, constantly on senior manager's lips and at the top of the board's agenda. Then we got a new board chairman and safety slid down the agenda.

What message did this send to staff at every level? That safety was sorted and other things were of higher priority? There was, immediately, a disconnect between how the management spoke and how the board acted. Thankfully, after an intervention, safety was again placed at the top of the board's monthly meeting agenda. It was, once again, everyone's top priority. There was no longer any possible misunderstanding.

It behoves every management team to constantly drive home to the staff what is considered important in that organisation. They must not sit back and believe that, if it is said at senior and middle management meetings, it will automatically be heard and acted upon by the staff down the chain.

Chapter Five

THE MAIN THING IS TO KEEP THE MAIN THING THE MAIN THING

This is a well-known quote by Stephen Covey, author of "The Seven Habits of Highly Effective People" and, was worldwide, a highly sought after and highly regarded writer and speaker on leadership.

I had the good fortune and honour, as Toastmasters International President in 2004, to be able to spend a fascinating hour of conversation alone with him, prior to the function at which I presented him with the Toastmasters International Golden Gavel Award. This is an award presented annually to a non-Toastmaster who has achieved prominence in the communication and leadership fields.

The point of the quote is both simple and obvious, but all too often rarely done. We all have goals in our lives and careers, but do we write them down and refer to them regularly?

As the saying goes, do we take steps to achieve them, or do we put them on the long finger?

Do we break our goals into smaller ones and achieve each part one by one?

As is often said, you need to get from point A to point B before moving to C and eventually, to Z, your goal.

Or, do we get distracted and divert our attention to the many and varied challenges that we encounter in our daily lives?

For example, when we go on the internet to find some information, do we go directly to that source? Or do we find something else that arouses our interest along the way, so that after 20 or 30 minutes, we eventually find what we set out for in the first place?

And don't get me started about Facebook!

Always remember the main thing is to keep the main thing the main thing.

Chapter Six

YOU CAN BEAT EGGS, BUT YOU CAN'T BEAT EXPERIENCE

Growing up in the countryside, like I did, people had all kinds of wise sayings like the title of this lesson. The meaning is obvious. A person may have all the degrees and qualifications you can count on ten fingers, yet not be as successful as someone with more experience.

Experience can be defined as something personally encountered, undergone, or lived through. As we're not born with experience, it's obviously something that happens during our journey through life. Whether good or bad experiences, we can learn from them, if we choose to do so. Often, people can be heard expressing it in the following fashion after serving in some position, or completing a project, or trying something new. They say: "If I only knew when I started what I know now, I would have done things differently." This is often expressed with a tinge of regret, seeing it through a negative lens, rather than recognising the extra learning and personal growth that has taken place.

Unfortunately, some people never learn from their experiences, doomed to make the same mistakes over and over again.

This old, quite ungrammatical quote comes to mind.

"If you do what you've always done, you'll get what you've always gotten."

If you wish to learn from your experiences, why not keep a diary or journal of the lessons learned from events, incidents, meetings, and other interactions. No need to write essays. Just note the things that went well and the things that could have been improved. Always be aware you can learn more by watching what is not working well, rather than when everything is going smoothly.

These notes will help you remember these learnings later.

And, finally, keep in mind that to beat eggs properly, you do need experience.

Chapter Seven

THE WAY WE DO THINGS AROUND HERE

How would you describe the culture of your organisation, business or office?

The following is a standard description:

"An organisation's culture consists of the values, beliefs, attitudes, and behaviours that employees share and use on a daily basis in their work. The culture determines how employees describe where they work, how they understand the business, and how they see themselves as part of the organisation."

If you consider this to be on the complicated side, let me quote a simpler definition.

The Confederation of British Industry describes culture as follows:

"…the mix of shared values, attitudes and patterns of behaviour that give the organisation its particular character. Put simply, it is "the way we do things around here."

Cultures are created organically or through deliberate action over time. Culture can't be changed overnight but needs consistent focus and attention from leadership, as cultural change is never a bottom-up event. Sometimes, this change is forced on organisations because of business failure, a take-over, or a series of serious accidents causing loss of life. Other times, more positively, it happens because of a change of leadership.

Judge Hand, in the Supreme Court of Massachusetts, way back in 1942, got it right when he said:

"We accept the verdict of the past until the need for change cries out loudly enough to force upon us a choice between the comforts of further inertia and the irksomeness of action."

Doesn't this sum it up very well? We are all inclined to do nothing until we are forced to make a choice between the comforts of doing nothing and the trouble of taking some action.

So, whether for good or otherwise, is the culture in your organisation "the way we do things around here?" Does that make you happy or sad? What can you do about it or does the "irksomeness of action" win out?

Chapter Eight

ARE YOU A MONKEY COLLECTOR?

"No, I do not work in the jungle collecting monkeys for some zoo, so how can this question apply to me." you respond.

But wait a minute. Have you read the book entitled, "The One Minute Manager Meets the Monkey," published in 1985 by Ken Blanchard, William Oncken and Hal Burrows?

It tells the story of the overworked and overwhelmed manager who, daily, works very long hours and – on many occasions - weekends. One Saturday, when he should have been at home with his family, he is instead seated at his desk staring at the pile of work in front of him. "What am I going to do with all this," he asked himself. "Will it ever stop?"

As he contemplated his desk and his dim future, he happened to look out the office window. There, across the street, was a golf course. And there, on the tee box, he espied four golfers, who at a closer glance, he recognised as four of his staff.

And that was his light bulb moment. "Hey," he said, "they should be in here attending to the work on my desk and I should be at home with my children!"

As a manager, at any level, it's very easy to collect problems i.e. monkeys from the staff.

Leave it to me; I'll take care of that; I'll call so and so and ask him/her for you are just some of the monkey collecting habits of overworked managers. There are many other examples.

What the manager is doing is taking an unsolved problem from a subordinate. When managers do that, they are allowing a monkey (figuratively) to leap from the employee's back on to their backs. This can substantially increase the manager's work load; but they also lose the opportunity to develop the subordinate, with the result that if the problem repeats itself, it will again fall to the manager to solve it.

In a classic article in the Harvard Business Review in 1974, authors William Oncken, Jr., and Donald L. Wass offer a theoretical framework for opening the eyes of today's leaders. In the article "Who's Got the Monkey?", the authors tell the tale of an overburdened manager who allows his employees to delegate upward.

Oncken and Wass offer a well-defined basic law for managing monkeys. It is:

- At no time while I am helping you, will your problem become my problem. Because the instant your problem becomes mine, you will no longer have a problem.

- You may ask my help at any appointed time, and we will make a joint determination of what the next move will be with your problem and who will make it.

- Refusing to accept problems that subordinates try to delegate upward, and instead giving them opportunities to meet with you to "feed the monkey" is the best choice for both the monkey and for its keeper. ("Feeding the monkey" in this case means offering advice, giving direction and enabling the employee to solve the problem.)

- The employee who is closest to the problem usually has the knowledge and skill to solve the problem, if empowered to do so.

So, your move, or the next move by your employee? It's your choice, because you're the "keeper."

Chapter Nine

THE LONE RANGER MANAGER

The "monkey collector" manager reminds me of the TV character, The Lone Ranger, played mostly by Clayton Moore in the TV series of the same name that aired on the USA ABC network from 1949 to 1957.

Together with his loyal helper, Tonto, they responded to crises in various western USA towns caused by lawless elements. They rode in, the masked Lone Ranger on his beautiful white stallion, Silver, quickly took control of the situation and sorted out the baddies to the satisfaction of the townspeople. They then left town as quickly as they had arrived, riding off into the sunset in a flurry of dust and the sound of galloping hooves.

However, there was no guarantee that if the problem reoccurred, the Lone Ranger and Tonto would be at hand to solve it. This was because, more than likely, they were off dealing with other lawless elements elsewhere. (I just love that description "lawless elements." What a nice way to describe bad behaviour!)

And that is exactly what happens, when the manager sorts out the staff's problems for them. Instead of coaching the staff to solve the problem themselves, the manager solves the problem for them. The problem is that the next time this particular problem occurs, it will again fall to the manager to deal with it.

A definition of coaching can be expressed as the art of inspiring, energising and facilitating the performance, learning and development of the person being coached.

Of course, coaching takes time but it's an investment that pays off, because over time, the staff become competent and confident in dealing with whatever challenges that come their way.

Then it's time for the manager to say, "Hi-Yo Silver, away!"

Chapter Ten

THE PARETO PRINCIPLE

You may not be aware of this principle by name, but likely you are aware of the 80/20 rule. Well, they're the same thing: it's also known as the law of the vital few.

In the late 19th century, Vilfredo Pareto (1848-1923), an Italian engineer, sociologist and economist, among other things, noticed that 80% of the land in Italy was owned by about 20% of the population.

He developed the principle by observing that about 20% of the peapods in his garden contained 80% of the peas.

Over time, it came to be accepted that roughly 80% of effects come from 20% of the causes.

Later, it became a common principle in business management that 80% of sales come from 20% of customers.

In any situation, a limited number of issues are likely to have the most impact.

The Pareto Principle helps separate the critical few from the non-critical, or even trivial, many. It is a simple, but very important concept for quality improvement, and for time management.

Turned on its head, it means someone can spend 80% of their valuable time chasing the ever decreasing 20% yet to be achieved. This is known as the law of diminishing returns. Perfectionists find this very difficult to resist, but resist they must, for otherwise they can spend their lives chasing the unachievable.

I once asked a member of my staff, who had wandered in to my office, had he heard of the 80/20 rule. After he answered in the negative, I explained what it was and how it worked. Then I asked him how he would describe his own approach. "I'm a 100/100 person," (meaning he would spend 100% of his time in order to achieve 100% perfection) he responded. And to tell you the truth, he had never spoken a truer word!

Chapter Eleven

IS YOUR SONG STILL UNSUNG?

The Indian poet and playwright, Tagore, born in the mid-19th century, once wrote: "I have spent my days stringing and unstringing my instrument, while the song I came to sing remains unsung."

Surely this is an excellent metaphor for unrealised potential?

Why do so many people with great potential waste their time in trivial pursuits, making little progress towards their goals and saying no to every growth and leadership opportunity?

The terrible pity is that unless they change, their songs will die with them.

But what about you?

- Does your bucket list get longer, rather than shorter?
- Do you realise your dreams are still your possibilities?

- Do you always say yes to growth and leadership opportunities?

When will you stop stringing and unstringing your instrument and begin to sing what is your unique song? When will you begin to welcome and accept the many opportunities that come your way as you navigate through life? When will you stop thinking and just start doing?

Not every one of these will work out positively, but nothing ventured is nothing gained.

Sometimes, it needs a friend, mentor or colleague to point out our possibilities. I could safely bet that almost everyone has had that experience. I certainly had.

Or, we're thrust into a situation where we're confronted with a yes/no question. Say yes and a whole new world reveals itself. Say no and you remain in your comfort zone and …… nothing changes. This is your moment of truth! What do you do when faced with a question like this?

I've often described it as like being in a room, doing well and happy with your lot, when suddenly a door slightly opens into an adjoining room. You can't fully see in, but you realise there is some exciting challenge there for you. You hesitate and think. Will I go in? Can I handle this challenge? Am I good enough?

Self-doubt affects us all. Faced with the unknown, our first reaction is always to hesitate. But then this friend, mentor or colleague pushes you and you're inside the room before you know it. And guess what? You quickly discover there was nothing to be fearful about. In fact, you adjust to the challenge extremely well and quickly and are well able to handle whatever needs doing. Your leadership skills increase to match the need. After some time, and once more you are still doing well and happy with your lot, when another door opens in the next room and the same process happens all over again. Once more you are faced with giving a yes/no answer, or you wait until you're pushed.

Shakespeare, born around 450 years ago, put it well in his play, Julius Caesar, when Brutus, on the high seas and faced with a major decision, exclaimed to his shipmates:

"There is a tide in the affairs of men, which taken at the flood leads on to fortune.

Omitted, all the voyage of their life is bound in shallows and in miseries.

On such a full sea are we now afloat and must take the current where it serves, or lose our ventures."

The meaning is self-evident. We either take the opportunities presented to us and enjoy success or turn our back on them and live to regret it. In other words, the tide of opportunity will have ebbed without us.

Now is the time, as Tagore describes it, to stop stringing and unstringing your instrument and begin to sing the song you were put on this world to sing. I can assure you the world is waiting.

I started this piece with a quote from him; I'll now end with another one from him.

"Everything comes to us that belongs to us, if we create the capacity to receive it."

You better believe it.

Chapter Twelve

DO OR DO NOT.
THERE IS NO TRY

I'm writing this piece the week the latest Star Wars movie, Star Wars: The Last Jedi, has opened in cinemas worldwide. I'm delighted that fabulous Irish scenery features in it, like it did in the previous release.

A long time ago in a galaxy far, far away, Yoda became a Jedi Grand Master and it's reported that, over the several centuries since, he's had a hand in training every Jedi in the galaxy. What an unbeatable and remarkable record that is; a record very unlikely to be matched!

With that galactic experience and stardust background, his advice, and indeed orders, must be heeded.

"Do or do not. There is no try," is one of his better-known exhortations.

It's simple and very direct. Saying you will try to do something indicates to everyone, including yourself, that there is a doubt you will succeed. Negative thoughts like this are not a great precursor of success. But, how often do we fall into this trap? I know I used to, but while serving on the Board of Toastmasters International, a colleague called me out on it every time I said it. He was a Yoda fan, naturally, and proud of it.

So, when asked to do something, consider if it's within your capacity to deliver, or not.

Then do, or do not. Forget about trying.

Continue to "try" and the Empire may Strike Back!

Chapter Thirteen

MANAGING VERSUS DOING

Do you spend enough of your time on management-type activities? Many managers find that much of their time is still taken up with the kinds of tasks they carried out before their promotion.

You can be sure you are managing if the bulk of your time is spent on deciding matters like the following.

a. What is to be achieved?
b. What work needs doing to achieve the desired outcomes?
c. How the work will be done?
d. When must the work be done by?
e. Who on your team will do the work?
f. How can you encourage your team to do the work well?
g. What resources will the team need to do the work?
h. How well the work is being done?
i. What action needs to be taken if things are not going to plan?

In short, you are managing if you are:

a. <u>Planning</u> the results to be obtained from your team's work – (a) above
b. <u>Organising</u> them to get the necessary work done – (b-f) above
c. <u>Resourcing</u> the team to get the work done – (g) above
d. <u>Monitoring</u> the outcomes of that work – (h) above
e. <u>Reviewing</u> progress and correcting slippages from the plan, or taking advantage of new opportunities – (i) above

"He who fails to plan, plans to fail." Anon

Chapter Fourteen

A MEETING IS AN EVENT WHERE MINUTES ARE KEPT AND HOURS ARE WASTED

We've all been at meetings at work, and elsewhere, that didn't start or finish on time, meandered all over the place and ended with no clear idea of what had been decided, or who was to do what and when. The result? Lots of very dissatisfied attendees.

These kinds of meeting are, regrettably, too frequent. Here are 10 suggestions to make the meetings you chair more interesting and constructive:

1. Have a written agenda, which has been circulated in advance.
2. Have clear objectives that are realistic, focused and measurable.
3. Ensure agenda items are introduced with positive language, such as "develop," "decide," or "recommend." Action words like these focus the attendees on outcomes.
4. Start and end on time. It's surprising how many meetings end on time when this is printed on the

agenda. Starting on time rewards the attendees who made the effort to show up on time.

5. Decide at the outset how much time will be devoted to each agenda item so that the meeting can end at the stated time. Doing this concentrates minds wonderfully.

6. Follow the agenda. Stay on track and disallow deviations.

7. Decide actions to be taken, by whom and by when.

8. Minutes of the meeting should record the decisions as outlined in #7.

9. Hold the meeting in a suitable place in terms of size, accessibility and free from possible disturbances.

10. Never forget that, as Chair, it's up to you to ensure a successful, productive and enjoyable meeting.

You may never arrive at a situation where attendees look forward, joyfully, to the next meeting. But, when they do turn up, they know decisions will be made. Progress is palpable and the attendees leave the meeting satisfied that you, the Chair, knew how to chair a meeting.

Chapter Fifteen

"UNTIL WE CAN MANAGE TIME, WE CAN MANAGE NOTHING ELSE"

These wise words are Peter F. Drucker's (1909-2005) who was an Austrian-born American management consultant and author who was a leader in management education.

Time is a manager's greatest enemy and managing time can be the greatest challenge. The ability to manage time is often what separates good managers from poor ones. If we can't organise ourselves, how can we be trusted to organise others! Yet, few of us manage time as well as we should - we can get distracted by jobs that are more interesting than the priority ones we should be attending to first.

Here are three basic ways of using time more effectively:

1. Cut out certain tasks.

2. Work more efficiently.

3. Plan the use of your time better.

One way to make better use of your time is to stop doing jobs you shouldn't be doing. Also stop doing work that really isn't worth doing, or just as well done by others.

The following are the key questions to ask.

- Have I a detailed job description?
- Do I know what my goals and priorities are?
- Do I know the best sequence to do what must be done?
- Am I doing work that can be delegated to others?
- Am I doing things that needn't be done at all?
- Do I spend enough of my time doing things that must be done and only I can do?

If your answers aren't what you know they should be, then you will know what to change.

In summary, there are four key requirements for good time management:

- Clear objectives.
- Forward planning.
- Ability to prioritise and focus on action.
- Ability to delegate successfully.

"The key is in not spending time, but in investing it."
Stephen R. Covey

Chapter Sixteen

PAYING THE PRICE

When Nelson Bunker Hunt, an USA oil millionaire in the early 20th century, was asked what his secret of success was, this was his answer:

"First you must decide what it is you want to achieve, then decide you're willing to pay the price to achieve it and finally pay the price."

Mr. Hunt's advice is so simple, yet so often not followed.

How often do people think about doing something, but never make a decision to do so? Thinking and rethinking something is not the same thing as deciding to do something. Deciding is the essential first step.

Having taken this vital first step, the next step is to decide that you're willing to pay the price to achieve your goal. Every decision you make has a price, either in time, cost, resources, or personal stress. Are you willing to pay this price?

Many people fall at this hurdle. The personal costs for proceeding to execute the decision outweigh, in their minds, the positives.

Having decided willingness to pay the price, the third and crucial step is to exactly do that.

Most people who have got past step #2, will go on to step #3. But the big test of commitment, concentration, indeed courage, begins here. People may begin paying the price but do they persevere to the end?

Nothing worth achieving was ever achieved easily. But, as Mr. Hunt so succinctly puts it, it will never get done unless you pay the price.

Chapter Seventeen

THE EISENHOWER METHOD

In a 1954 speech to the Second Assembly of the World Council of Churches, the then U.S. President Dwight D. Eisenhower said:

"I have two kinds of problems: the urgent and the important. The urgent are not important, and the important are never urgent."

Does his statement resonate with you? Do you find yourself chasing the urgent but not important to the detriment of making progress on the important but not urgent items?

If you do, welcome to the club.

To complicate matters further for us, there are two other categories of priority which must be dealt with – "important and urgent" and "not important and not urgent."

Here are the four categories in order of priority:

1. "Important and urgent."
   Means drop everything and do it now. You can't afford to hang around and risk the consequences.

2. "Important but not urgent."
    The temptation is to leave these tasks until "tomorrow." For most of us tomorrow never comes.
3. "Urgent but not important."
    These are the tasks you need to delegate to someone else, but, more often than not, fail to do so! In many cases, these are somebody else's tasks which have been delegated to you. Hard luck!
4. "Not important and not urgent."
    It is very easy to busy yourself with such tasks, all the while convincing yourself that you're working very hard. No matter how much time you spend at these tasks, there will always be more to do. It's a never-ending street. Yet, here is often where we find ourselves, because we can't resist the temptation.

How many times have you checked your mobile phone already today?

The lesson from #2 on the list is that important tasks, which have no immediate urgency, must not be left aside until you find time to attend to them. Rather, you must make the time to attend to them, because, if you don't, you will wake up one morning and they will have become important and urgent. Then it may be too late.

Chapter Eighteen

YOU MUST LISTEN TO THUNDER

You must listen to thunder was another favourite saying of my grandmothers. It was her way of saying that when people are expressing various opinions contrary to yours, rather than waste time arguing against them, in most cases, just listen and let their arguments wash over your head.

This was a good strategy. Attempting to win arguments about very minor matters is an exercise in futility. Yet, how many of us do this? And the result? Both sides remain unmoved. Stress levels are increased. Friendships are strained. And for what?

It takes two to tango as the saying goes. Argumentative people are ten-a-penny, often speaking from deeply held convictions. Other times they speak, not from any real knowledge about the subject, but from an emotional state. Their minds and views are not for changing and it's completely pointless attempting to do so.

Unfortunately, however, our egos can get in the way compelling us to continue the argument until we have won it, or think we've won it. Then what? Has the world changed in some way?

Better save your energy, keep your blood pressure levels steady and, like my grandmother, just listen to the thunder. Like all thunderstorms, this too will pass.

Chapter Nineteen

DON'T LET THE LITTLE THINGS GET YOU!

Albert Reynolds (1932-2014) was Taoiseach (Prime Minister) of Ireland from 1992 to 1994. Even though he served for just a few years, he has two major achievements to his name. One was the part he played in the signing of the Anglo-Irish Agreement in 1993, which was the turning point in the much-desired peace process in the long-running conflict in Northern Ireland.

Secondly, during his term of office, Reynolds negotiated considerable benefits for Ireland from the European Union regional aid budget, a sum which is estimated to have amounted to 7 billion euro. These were two big major achievements.

And then, in 1994, the unthinkable happened. His coalition partners in Government withdrew their support, the Government collapsed, a general election was held and when the dust had settled, Mr Reynolds was no longer Taoiseach.

His coalition partners had finally withdrawn their support because of revelations of tardiness in the Attorney

General's office in processing an issue which had lain dormant in that office for an unacceptable period of time.

Just one "mislaid" letter had led to his eventual downfall and loss of high office.

He went to his grave remembered for him saying, after losing office, and no doubt with a tinge of regret, "You get the big things right, and then a little thing gets you."

What a lesson this is for all of us. More often than not, while we're concentrating on the big things, something little can come out of nowhere and cause us distress, injury, or loss.

This can be a health issue, a business issue, a people issue – indeed, take your choice of issues.

For example, you can be a careful accident free car driver for years and years and then, while casually glancing at your phone one day, you have a serious accident. You got the big things (safe driving) right for years and then the little matter of glancing at your phone got you.

Albert was right. You can get the big things right but, if you're not careful, a little thing can get you.

Better watch out!

Chapter Twenty

ARE YOU DONE YET?

Every now and again, it can be our good fortune to meet someone who is truly remarkable. It happened to me at the Toastmasters International Convention in Atlanta, Georgia, USA in August 2003.

It's a story I never tire of telling.

At the luncheon hosted by me for 76 incoming District Governors, I met a most extraordinary human being.

His name was Charlie Keane and he was the District Governor of District 31, comprising the whole of Massachusetts, USA. We made some small talk and, as he looked rather elderly, my curiosity was aroused.

I said, "do you mind if I ask you what age you are?"

"Not at all, I was 98 years old last July 19," he replied.

I was speechless! A 98-year-old man a District Governor, with all the responsibilities that role entails. Quickly, regaining my senses I asked him: "Do you have a motto or life theme?"

"My motto," he replied, is, "I'm not done yet."

I'm-not-done-yet, at age 98!

I met him again near Boston the following June, just a month short of his 99th birthday. He came to meet me at Logan Airport (no, he wasn't driving) and, at a function the next morning, he gave a 5-minute speech without any notes and without stumbling over his words. He would have put someone half his age to shame. When the Toastmasters recognition results for the year were announced in July 2004, the District 31 team led by Charlie had achieved all their goals; an unprecedented achievement. Charlie lived to be 103, a truly remarkable man and an example for all of us.

His message is simple. Never, never, tell yourself you're too old - or it's too late - to begin something new and exciting.

You're certainly not done yet!

Chapter Twenty-one

IF YOU AREN'T FIRED WITH ENTHUSIASM, YOU WILL BE FIRED, WITH ENTHUSIASM

The Green Bay Packers, an American football team, was founded on August 11, 1919 by Curly Lambeau and George Whitney Calhoun in the city of Green Bay, Wisconsin, USA. Lambeau solicited funds for uniforms from his employer, the Indian Packing Company and was given money for uniforms and equipment, hence the name Packers. The Packers still play in Lambeau Field, named, in 1965, after his death, in memory of Curly.

The 1919 season was their first season of competitive football and since then the club has won 13 league championships, including 4 Super Bowls.

The history of the club is not, however, one of unbridled success.

Prior to the arrival of Vince Lombardi as head coach in 1959, the Packers had gone through a lengthy, lean period. And then everything changed.

The Packers of the 1960s became one of the most dominant American football teams of all time.

Having taken over a last-place team in 1959, Lombardi built it into a juggernaut, winning five league championships over a seven-year span culminating with victories in the first two Super Bowls.

What was his secret? How was he able to mould a team broken down by defeats and failures into a team that won all before them? He did it by the force of his personality, managing, very quickly, to achieve individual commitment to a group effort. This was what he believed in:

"Individual commitment to a group effort - that is what makes a team work, a company work, a society work, a civilization work."

Lombardi was a man who did not suffer fools gladly, nor did he suffer players who didn't buy into his philosophy.

Defeat in games was never an option. The possibility of losing never entered the players' minds after quotes like the following were hammered into their heads.

"It's not whether you get knocked down, it's whether you get up."

"Once you learn to quit, it becomes a habit."

Do you instil confidence in your team? Do they believe in you? Would they, as the saying goes, run through a brick wall for you?

Why not? And what are you going to do about it?

I was thrilled, in 2003, to be given a tour of Lambeau Field and the Packer's head office. I was even invited to

Lombardi's office and allowed to sit in his chair. As I gazed around this revered place at all the memorabilia adorning the walls, I thought of the man who came here as a relative unknown and left as probably the most famous coach in football.

He achieved this success through his outstanding communication and leadership qualities, combined with an iron will, strong discipline and making it clear to everyone in the club that:

"If you aren't fired with enthusiasm, you will be fired, with enthusiasm."

Has a simple comma ever made such a difference?

Chapter Twenty-two

ALL OF IT!

The Rockefeller name is one of the most recognisable business names in the USA and indeed, farther afield.

John D. Rockefeller was born July 8, 1839, in Richford, New York. He built his first oil refinery near Cleveland and in 1870 incorporated the Standard Oil Company. By 1882, he had a near-monopoly of the oil business in the USA. Late in life, Rockefeller devoted himself to philanthropy and his money helped found various Institutes and Foundations. In total, he is reputed to have given away more than $530 million to various causes, before passing away in 1937 at age 98.

The story is told, more than likely an apocryphal one, about a journalist from the Wall Street Journal, after Rockefeller's death, deciding to write about his life. While gathering the necessary information, he called Rockefeller's lawyer and asked him how much he, Rockefeller, had left. Thinking the answer would be millions and millions of dollars, he was taken considerably aback when the lawyer's response, after a brief pause, was "all of it."

Whether the story is true or false, the bottom line that everyone knows, is that we can't take money, or possessions, with us when we die.

So, the question then is why are some people so greedy? Is enough ever enough? No matter where you live, or how expensive your lifestyle, there is still only 24 hours in the day to spend your money. Does being very rich make a person happier? I can't say, as I don't fall into that category.

What I can say is that helping other people through my membership in Toastmasters International and Rotary International makes me happier, as I know my efforts, aggregated with thousands of others, can make a big difference in people's lives.

All this takes for me is some spare time with very little cost involved.

What do you do with your time to make the world a better place?

After we pass on, if, or when, a journalist asks how much we left and the answer is "all of it," let's hope it won't be money that's being referred to, but the positive results of the time we spent helping others.

Chapter Twenty-three

THERE IS NO "I" IN TEAM

A common definition of a team is a group of people who work together to accomplish specific common goals.

Most of us have been on a team at some stage of our lives.

Some teams were very productive, some couldn't wait until our term was over, if, indeed we lasted that long.

What was the difference?

Well, the productive ones had the following:

- ✓ A leader.
- ✓ Clear purpose.
- ✓ Clear goals.
- ✓ Clear timeline.
- ✓ Shared responsibility.
- ✓ Ability to get the job done.
- ✓ An agreed process for making decisions.
- ✓ Decisions fully accepted and supported.
- ✓ No prima donnas.

In other words, team members know:

- ✓ What they are to accomplish.
- ✓ Why they are doing it.
- ✓ How to do it.
- ✓ When it is to be completed.
- ✓ The process for arriving at decisions.

Something that's often overlooked is an agreed process for making decisions. When this agreed process is missing, discussions can go on for far longer than necessary. A fairly typical situation is where every team member, bar one, is in agreement on an issue. Then an argument rages to persuade the hold-out member to accept the majority view, which often can lead to strife and bad feelings, not to mention the waste of time.

All this can be avoided if the rules are agreed at the start i.e. a majority vote carries the day.

This process also deals with the prima donna (the "I" person) mentioned earlier, who believes they are special and have to have the last word on everything.

When I was elected chairman of the Council of my golf club, I was determined that the monthly meeting would last two hours and no longer. As previous history had indicated, this was more honoured in the breach than in the observance, often caused by one or more different individuals attempting to force their opinion on the others and not conceding to the majority view.

At the first meeting, I proposed to the other Council members that:

a) The meeting would end after two hours.

b) Decisions would be made by majority vote after a reasonable time for discussion, depending on the issue.

This proposal was accepted unanimously and each meeting, thereafter, started and ended on time.

We acted as a united team with the good of the club at heart.

Accordingly, there was no "I" on our team.

Chapter Twenty-four

IF YOU CAN READ, YOU CAN LEARN

John (Sonny) Guerin was my mother's first cousin. According to my grandmother's diary, his aunt, he left his widowed mother's home for the last time, on December 19, 1924 to live with his uncle Dan in Sydney, Australia. His passage having been paid for by Dan, he sailed from London on the Barrowbool P&O on December 22, 1924. Aged just 17½, he was fated never to see his country, his home, or his mother, again.

Despite his great distance from Ireland, he was to play a major role in my life. Growing up in a small cottage without electricity, any kind of books were in short supply. But, a number of times a year, a large box of books, postmarked Sydney, would be delivered to my cottage. These books covered a wide range of subject matter: history, travel, westerns, mostly factual, but some fictional. I cannot remember how I learned to read, but I read and read and read. Before I ever started school, I was well able to read.

In school, I found still another source of reading material, supplied by the Carnegie Library. A large wooden box, containing some 100 books, or more, would be delivered by truck every term and I would read every book in the box, often two a day.

The Carnegie Library in Ireland was funded by the Andrew Carnegie Foundation.

Andrew Carnegie was born in Dunfermline Scotland in 1835. When he was 13, he and his family moved to Pennsylvania. His first job in 1848 was changing spools of thread in a cotton mill 12 hours a day, 6 days a week, in a Pittsburgh cotton factory. His starting wage was $1.20 per week ($36.36 in 2017 dollars). From that humble beginning, Carnegie became the richest man in the America through, principally, his hugely successful steel businesses.

Before his death on August 11, 1919, Carnegie had donated $350M to various causes.

The "Andrew Carnegie Dictum" was:

- To spend the first third of one's life getting all the education one can.
- To spend the next third making all the money one can.
- To spend the last third giving it all away for worthwhile causes.

Among his many philanthropic efforts, the establishment of public libraries throughout the United States, Canada, Britain, Ireland, and other English-speaking countries was especially prominent.

He was motivated to do this by the fact, that as a young boy, he had access to a large collection of books owned by a Colonel James Anderson who lived near him in Allegheny, Pennsylvania.

Below are his thoughts on which is most important – mind or money:

"Man does not live by bread alone. I have known millionaires starving for lack of the nutriment which alone can sustain all that is human in man, and I know workmen, and many so-called poor men, who revel in luxuries beyond the power of those millionaires to reach.

It is the mind that makes the body rich. There is no class so pitiably wretched as that which possesses money and nothing else."

I thank these two generous men, people I never met, and wealth, worlds, and generations apart, who gave me a love of reading which has stood me in good stead to this day, proving the point that if you can read you can learn. And it is learning that makes the body rich.

Chapter Twenty-five
THE UNIVERSE ALWAYS ANSWERS

I've heard many people say over the years: put it out to the universe and the universe will answer. What was meant by this was the idea that, if you are struggling with a challenge, a problem, a trouble, then ask the universe and the solution will come to you. I regarded it as another new age idea which had no basis in fact but was rather our subconscious mind coming to our aid.

Several times, in the course of writing this book, I found myself stumped for the next line in a story, or piece. Stepping away from my desk for several minutes, or more, and then returning to the job at hand, nearly always resulted in more creativity. I put this down to allowing my subconscious work out the answer.

Then something strange and unexpected happened that caused me to change my mind.

But, let me start at the start.

Toastmasters International is comprised of more than 100 districts spread throughout the world. When a district grows to a certain size of clubs and members, it begins the task of reforming. This was about to happen in District 71

comprising all the U.K. and Ireland. Having been created in 1972, the district had now grown to a size when it needed to be reformed and split into two districts.

I thought it would be a good time to write the history of Toastmasters on these islands before the break-up happened. As someone who was involved in the affairs of the district, one way or another, since the mid 1980s, I had in my possession minutes of meetings, programs, correspondence, plus personal recollections to rely on. But, prior to the early '80s, practically nothing. Considering the first club in the U.K. was chartered in 1935 and in Ireland, 1958, this left a huge gap in this unique story.

I had come to a sudden stop with no solution in sight.

Then the Dublin club, the first Irish club, founded in 1958, invited me to speak at one of its regular weekly meetings in February 2012. I spoke about leadership and, inter alia, mentioned persistence as an invaluable trait in a leader. I referenced the club's founding father, Paddy Cunningham, as a wonderful example of persistence because of the struggles he endured to get the club chartered.

After the meeting, I caught the train home, opened my laptop and there staring me in the face was an email from Paddy's daughter Lisa. I hadn't seen or heard from Lisa for a number of years, so that was a surprise in itself. A far greater surprise was the content of her email asking me if I would be interested in her late father's collection of

Toastmasters materials which she found when cleaning out the attic.

You can guess how this ended can't you?

Suffice to say, I managed to write the complete history of District 71, from 1935 onwards, using the material from this irreplaceable treasure trove.

Was this a one in a million random event, or did the universe come to my rescue?

You be the judge.

Chapter Twenty-six

ARE YOU A TALKER OR A COMMUNICATOR?

People talk all the time; at home, at work, on the phone, wherever people gather.

At other times, people are required to give presentations and/or speak in a public forum. In your experience, how successful are they in communicating their message to their audience?

Is it very clear what the message is, backed up with facts and stories that catch and hold your attention?

Do you find yourself becoming emotionally connected to the speaker and their message?

Or, are you just as wise after the speaker ends, as you were before the start? If so, you have been listening to a talker, not a communicator.

There are three principle ways people communicate with each other.

These are through a conversation, through a written message, either paper or electronic, or through a speech to an audience, large or small. Communicating through conversation, or the written word, differs from a speech in a very fundamental way.

In a conversation, questions can be asked and answered by either side until each party is clear what is being communicated. It can be described as the receipt by one side of information sent by the other side and vice versa. And, of course, fully understood by both sides.

Something that is written can be read and reread as many times as necessary until the message and meaning becomes clear.

How many chances does one get to understand the message and purpose of an in-person speech?

The answer, I'm afraid, is just a single chance! When the speaker ends and you haven't got their message, you don't get a second chance. The speech has disappeared into the ether, or wherever old speeches go, never to be seen again.

Earlier this year, my Rotary club invited a director of a well-known not-for-profit organisation in Dublin to speak at our weekly lunch. Well dressed and well spoken, he confidently addressed us for 20 minutes about his business. Immediately he was seated, I asked my friend David, who was sitting beside me: "David, can you tell me three things the speaker said?" David thought for about ten seconds, turned to me and said: "Ted, I can't tell you one thing he said, never mind three."

We had been listening to a talker, not to someone who communicated, and because of that, it turned out to be a complete waste of his time and ours.

I bet you've had that experience? Too often, you say.

Toastmasters International has trained over four million people in communication and leadership skills, since its foundation in 1924. As a member, you learn how to organise a speech which has a clear purpose to either inform, persuade, inspire or entertain. You learn how to put your support material together with a clear opening, body and conclusion. Your important message can then be heard and understood by everyone.

Armed with these skills, every time you speak you will be a communicator, never just a talker.

Chapter Twenty-seven

A MILLION TO ONE CHANCE, OR WAS IT EVEN GREATER?

Have you ever pulled a "sickie? A sickie in Ireland is calling in sick to work when you're not sick at all, but feeling tired, maybe a bit out of sorts, or, just admit it, a little lazy. Or, perhaps you go and have your car serviced, because you don't want to waste your precious weekend. In other words, call it what is, you're on the dodge from work.

Have you ever pulled two sickies in succession i.e. two days consecutively? Probably not as often.

Have you ever pulled two consecutive sickies and the next day went on a two weeks' vacation?

If you did, you probably travelled to some foreign shore and relaxed in the sun, sand and sea, far away from the stresses of work and removed from the tender mercies of your boss, knowing it would be two whole weeks before you had to face work again.

On such thoughts, dreams are founded, and carefree holidays are anticipated. But, sometimes, they don't work out quite like that.

As the old English proverb says:

"There's many a slip 'twixt cup and the lip." You're about to find out how true that is!

Back in the '80s, when our two daughters Sinéad and Claire were still in their early teens, my wife, Celine, and I, with the girls, went on holiday to Spain, Italy and France over various years that decade. Air travel back then was still horrendously expensive, but, as an employee of Irish Rail, my family and I had a limited amount of free and reduced travel annually on other railways and ferries.

By rail and ferry, a journey to Spain took two days and two nights each way. But what a way to see Wales, England, London, Paris and France on the way. The girls were exposed to foreign travel at an early age, an interest they still pursue.

Arriving back early one morning at the station Gare du Nord, one of the main railway stations in Paris, after a 12-hour overnight couchette train journey from Spain, we had a three-hour break before catching the train to Calais on the next leg of our long journey home. Although tired, the girls were still eager for adventure." Daddy, Daddy." they cried, "please show us the Metro." I resisted their pleas for a while but eventually gave in to their entreaties.

We descended via several escalators to the bowels of the station and eventually found ourselves in a large circular area with passageways running off it in several directions. At around 8 a.m. this was in the middle of the morning rush with hundreds of people scampering hither and thither.

On one wall of this large area, I espied a very big map of the Metro. Thinking this would be a clever time-saving way of showing the children what it looked like, we went over and gazed at the map. A young man was standing directly in front of us, also intently studying the map. Suddenly, without any warning, he stepped back, turned around, and exclaimed, "Jeez, it's Mr. Corcoran." Recognising him immediately as one of my staff from back home in Dublin, I said, "Tommy (not his real name), what are you doing here?" "I'm sick," was his amazing response. It turned out that he was on his way to Yugoslavia, also by train and ferry, and had taken two "sickies" as travel days, before enjoying his two weeks in the sun. He had not just taken two days, but two days at one of the busiest weekends of the year.

What to do? I was still on my holidays – Tommy was beginning his. Should I tell him to report to my office on his return where I would deal with his unauthorised absence and, in the meantime, spoil his holiday with the sword of Damocles hanging over him. Or warn him there and then never to do this again and that would be the end of the matter?

Because I'm a nice person at heart (!), after a split second's thought, I did the latter and we parted company. After ten seconds, or less, I thought of a question about something back home, I knew he could answer. I turned around but he had completely disappeared into the raging throng of commuters rushing to and fro. It was as if it all had been a dream.

What were the chances of meeting a "sick" member of my staff in the bowels of a crowded Metro station in Paris, miles and miles from Ireland? A few seconds earlier or a few seconds later, for either of us, and I wouldn't be telling you this story.

A million to one chance? Or was it even greater than that?

Chapter Twenty-eight

MEASURE TWICE, CUT ONCE

Originally, this was great advice for trainee tailors. No use finding you had the wrong measurements after the cloth had been cut. If you've heard this said in a general context, it was probably advice to plan and prepare properly before taking some action, or not rush making important decisions without first doing due diligence.

The following story will show how important this advice can be.

In his later years, my late father lived alone in a small cottage in Co. Kerry, Ireland. He kept a cow which grazed in the acre adjoining the cottage. Whether he developed illusions of becoming a big farmer, or not, he went and bought another cow. Now he had two mouths to feed and suddenly he had more milk than he could personally use. To bring the surplus to the local creamery, he decided to buy a donkey, tackling and cart. But this business expansion brought another problem; how could he feed three hungry animals on one acre?

The answer was renting an acre somewhere and letting the donkey graze there, when grass got short in the home place. A neighbour lived nearby in a cottage, also with an acre, and when he passed away, his brother, Jack, rented the grazing to Dad and the cottage to Max (not his real name), a pharmacist from London, and his wife and child, for the month of July each year. After enjoying his stay, and on returning home to London, Max purchased the cottage and, as he thought, the entire acre. Next year he and his family arrived back in Kerry to enjoy their summer break.

Looking out the first morning, he was surprised to see a donkey grazing on his property. He immediately wrote a curt letter to Jack, the seller of the acre, asking him to remove the donkey forthwith. Jack's response was startling. Max had not purchased the full acre, as he had imagined, but just half of it! He had failed to accurately check the map of his purchase and paid the price for his lack of attention. There was nothing he could do about it now.

His young daughter, however, saw the bright side. Falling in love with the donkey, she persuaded her rather rich father to buy the donkey and equipment from Dad for a goodly sum of money and then, for the remainder of the month, enjoyed her acquisition. But a day of reckoning was at hand. After the family's return to London, who would take care of the donkey for the next eleven months? The answer was obvious. So, Max returned to Dad and paid him to mind the donkey for the duration, as well as permitting him to use the animal and equipment meanwhile. And free grazing into the bargain.

A classic case, don't you agree of having your cake and eating it? Only in Ireland!

If Max had only measured twice before buying. If only.

Is there a lesson here for you?

Chapter Twenty-nine

THE MEITHEAL

If you haven't lived for a spell in the south or west of Ireland, you probably have no idea what a Meitheal is.

Meitheal is the Irish language word for a work team and denotes the system of co-operation in Ireland, that exists/existed in Ireland for probably hundreds of years, where groups of neighbours help each other, in turn, with farming work (although not exclusively), such as harvesting crops. A Meitheal is a wonderful example of the saying, "what goes around comes around," as, in Ireland, it is/was the traditional method for getting work done that couldn't be done on one's own. Your work one day – your neighbour's the next.

For me, growing up in Kerry in the '50s, the concept was everywhere. Back then, there was little or no farm machinery. What machinery did exist, needed a lot of extra man power to get the work done. So, work like hay making, threshing the corn, or crop harvesting, required more help than the farmers could provide from their own resources. Depending on the work being done, neighbours turned up to assist. Hay could be saved with the help of 4/5 extra people, but threshing corn could take 30, or more. The work involved could take hours, or even days.

On the day, neighbours turned up in the required numbers, secure in the knowledge that when their turn came, the necessary assistance would be forthcoming. Reciprocation was a given and no record was ever kept of the hours, or days, exchanged. All that mattered was that the work got done, as the weather window in an Irish summer can be short. The neighbours acted as a team of volunteers, no payment was asked for, or sought and everyone benefiting in one form or another.

When I moved to the city, aged 18, I missed this sense of belonging very much. No farms, neighbours who kept to themselves and a zero sense of community. Cities can be very lonely places for young country boys with little money, even while surrounded by the hustle and bustle of city life. When some years later, I moved to Dublin, things didn't change much. I became involved in various clubs and associations, but these didn't compensate for that sense of community I missed so much.

And then I joined a Toastmasters club and everything changed. Every member in such a club is on a personal journey of communication and leadership growth. One day someone is helping you – the next you are helping someone else. All of this help is given with a big heart and with no expectations.

It is, exactly, a modern version of the Meitheal that I had known and missed so much.

I had rediscovered what had mattered to me so much in my youth and it was, and still is, a wonderful feeling.

Chapter Thirty

LEADERSHIP IS ACTION, NOT POSITION

These are the words of Donald H. McGannon, a New Yorker, who was president of Westinghouse Broadcasting Company for more than 25 years.

In just five words, he nails it. Being in a leadership position does not, by default, make someone a leader. It's how the person acts in that position that makes the difference.

The news media is full every day with talk of leaders and leadership. But, how many of them are actually leading? As John C. Maxwell, an internationally recognised leadership expert, puts it so well:

"If you think you are leading and nobody is following, then you're only taking a walk."

In my experience, people in management positions fall into these three categories:

1. They lead and manage.
2. They manage only.
3. They neither lead nor manage.

I describe management as the "what" managers do.

The "what" can be described as planning, organising, implementing, facilitating, monitoring and reviewing.

To me, planning is the task that gets glossed over most often. People don't seem to know about the old adage which says: "One minute spent in planning can save three or four in execution." Yet, they hurry to the implementation stage without sufficient preparation and then wonder why things go awry. Another neglected area is reviewing progress and perhaps then tweaking the plan accordingly. Reviewing is most often associated with activities that didn't pan out as expected. However, it's equally important to review the activities that worked well. By reviewing both positive and negative outcomes, the team learns.

I describe leadership as the "how" leaders manage.

The "how" is about vision and having the ability to persuade team members it's worthwhile working towards it. Now the team has a "why." Leaders also make timely decisions and don't leave their teams waiting and waiting. They are supportive, they develop members and prepare them for further advancement. Importantly, they never overlook recognising good performance. Recognition rocks! Of my managers, the one I still remember with great affection and gratitude, is the one who supported me through thick and thin. Not just when everything was working well but, specifically, when it was the opposite.

Excellent leaders possess high levels of emotional intelligence which usually means they are personally and socially aware. They show empathy and are a joy to work for. They inspire greater and greater achievements.

In short, they believe that leadership is action, not position. That's why they're successful.

Chapter Thirty-one

IT'S NOT WHAT HAPPENS TO YOU....

The first time I saw or heard W. Mitchell was at a Toastmasters International Convention where he was a keynote speaker. Not knowing anything about him, I was surprised when he appeared on stage in a wheelchair, then moved across the stage before returning to the centre, all without uttering a word.

Now centre stage, he looked at us and said:

"It's not what happens to you, it's what you do about it."

If there was ever anyone who could be seen as an outstanding example of this advice, it was W. Mitchell.

His story is a sad, but inspiring one.

Having just completed his first solo aircraft flight, he was riding his motorcycle through San Francisco on July 19, 1971, when a truck turned in front of him. The gas cap on his Honda motorcycle came loose and Mitchell was enveloped in a wall of flames. Over 65% of his body was burned, with the greatest scarring on his face and hands and losing most of his ten fingers. He spent months in the hospital, where the staff were so concerned that he would be so distraught about his appearance, that mirrors were banned anywhere near him.

He was eventually discharged, went on to get a pilot's license and founded, with others, a very successful company. On November 11, 1975 as he was taking off from a small airport in Colorado, the small plane plummeted from about 100 feet, due to undetected ice on the wings, and he was left paralysed from the waist down. Fate decreed, that while his life was permanently changed, his travelling companions escaped injury.

This is how his website describes his life and career subsequently:

> *"Step by step, Mitchell moved forward with his life. He became an internationally acclaimed mayor "who saved a mountain", a successful business owner who put thousands of people to work, a congressional nominee from Colorado, and a respected environmentalist and conservationist who repeatedly testified before Congress. His accomplishments have received media recognition in North America on Good Morning America, The Today Show, NBC Nightly News and their counterparts around the world. He has been a radio and television host, a successful author, an award-winning international keynote speaker and the subject of numerous television specials."*

Beat that, says you!

He would put most of us who are reasonably able-bodied to shame with the range of his achievements.

I had a short chat with him after his convention keynote and found him a charming and interesting man who cheerfully signed a copy of his book for me.

As he's quoted. "Before I was paralysed there were 10,000 things I could do. Now there are 9,000. I can either dwell on the 1,000 I've lost or focus on the 9,000 I have left."

Truly, an inspiration to us all.

Chapter Thirty-two

MIND THE GAP

There are so many gaps in the world, you wouldn't know where to start.

Tell a farmer he's got a gap and immediately he'll begin to think of his fields.

Ask someone in Co. Kerry, Ireland, about the Gap and you'll be directed to the Gap of Dunloe.

Listen in Connolly Railway Station, Dublin, and you will hear the announcement, "Mind the Gap," warning people to mind the gap between the train and the platform. Despite these warnings, people still fall between them. You might well ask why such a gap is allowed to exist? Well, the answer is simple. While train carriages are usually approximately 20m in length and built in a straight line, many station platforms are curved, thus causing a greater or smaller gap at certain points. Hence the warning.

Have you gaps in your life?

Maybe a gap in your education and qualifications?

Maybe a gap in your experience?

Maybe a gap in your wider relationships?

Maybe a gap between your health checks?

Maybe a gap in your finances?

Maybe a gap in your communication and leadership skills?

When will you begin to fill these gaps, or will you, like the passenger in the train station, fall when you're least expecting it?

Then it will be, indeed, too late to heed the warning, "Mind the Gap."

Chapter Thirty-three

SIX DEGREES OF SEPARATION

Six degrees of separation is the idea that all living things and everything else in the world are six or fewer steps away from each other. So, the theory is you know someone, who knows someone, who knows someone, who knows someone, who knows someone, who knows anyone you can think of. The concept is absolutely amazing, but proven in several experiments worldwide to be factual, or nearly so.

You can "know" someone through various electronic media, including phones and never have met them.

But does it work if you substitute "meet" rather than "know?" I can't find any reason why it should not, but instinctively it seems a much more difficult achievement and, anyway, how can it be proven?

Sometimes life conspires in weird and wonderful ways. What are the chances that I was just two steps, not six, from President John F. Kennedy, his bothers Robert and Edward, and his sister Jean on disparate and separate occasions?

Let's start with JFK. A hero in Ireland, because of his Irish roots, who left a nation shocked and deeply grieving after his assassination. He visited here in June 1963 and left a lasting impression. During his stay, he visited Cork city where I was working at the time. In mid-afternoon, we all got off work and stood by the side of the street to watch him pass by very slowly in an open topped motor. He waved to the crowd as he passed, first one side, then the other side. It was hard to believe that less than six months later he was dead.

I don't claim this incident as personally meeting him, but I did meet his sister a number of times as she passed through Heuston Railway Station, Dublin, where I worked for a number of years. Jean Kennedy Smith served as the U.S. Ambassador to Ireland from 1993 to 1998.

In 2006, I spent a few days in Boston with my friend Tom. During my stay we were invited to lunch by a friend of his who turned out to have worked for Senator Robert Kennedy and had some personal interaction with his brother Senator Edward Kennedy.

During lunch, she told the story when, as someone newly working in Robert's office, he came downstairs on November 1, All Saints Day for Catholics, and asked her had she been at church that day. When she answered no, he offered to take her with him to Mass in Boston Cathedral. As they were running late, they stood at the back. When the collection was being taken up, Senator Kennedy leant over and asked her had she any money on her. She opened her purse and showed him a dime and a single quarter. He famously said: "I better take the quarter

– I'm a Kennedy." In disbelief, I said to her: "he hadn't any money!" Her reply was: "The Kennedys never had any money on them."

The following year, while at a dinner in Washington D.C., I was seated beside a lady I knew who had, for job reasons, recently moved with her husband from Hawaii to D.C. Feeling some sympathy with her on this major move, I asked her how she had coped with the change. She told me that she was born and raised in D.C. and actually worked there for a time. When asked what work she did there, she told me she worked for some time for Senator Robert Kennedy.

Can you imagine the chances, within 12 months of each other, separately meeting two women out of millions of citizens, who had worked for him!

So much for six degrees of separation – two degrees work fine for me!

Chapter Thirty-four

IT ALWAYS SEEMS IMPOSSIBLE UNTIL IT'S DONE

In May 2004, as Toastmasters International President, I had the pleasure of visiting South Africa with my daughter Claire. After the district conference in Johannesburg, we flew to Port Elizabeth and spent a few days there on safari. Next stop was Cape Town. Robben Island was a must-visit, so one day we embarked on the short sea trip. I was eager to see where Nelson Mandela had been incarcerated for 18 of the 27 years he served behind bars, before the fall of apartheid.

The island itself is tiny, just 3.3kms by 1.9kms and only 6.9kms from Cape Town. We were greeted by a former inmate who showed us Mandela's cell, just 7x7 feet in area, without even a bed, but some blankets on the floor to sleep on. And a slop bucket in the corner.

Next, we saw the yard where the prisoners worked every day breaking rocks with a small hammer. I just couldn't imagine how it must have felt sitting there in the hot sun, day after day, year after year, with no means of escape.

From the island there is clear sight to Cape Town and Table Mountain behind. Imagine constantly being aware of these iconic images of freedom for a long 18 years, yet remaining completely out of reach? Has anywhere ever seemed so near, yet so far? As a qualified lawyer, how demeaning it must have been to be confined in such conditions for so long.

Nevertheless, he referred to Table Mountain as a Beacon of Hope always clinging to the dream of one day being free.

His indomitable spirit never flinched, never succumbing to hatred and bitterness, even though while in prison, his mother and eldest son died and he was not permitted to attend their funerals.

He was confined to Robben Island from 1964 to 1982, before being moved, first to Pollsmoor prison in Cape Town and, later, to another prison where he stayed till his release on February 11, 1990.

Over a short time, the government and the ANC brokered a deal, which won Mandela and President FW de Klerk the Noble Peace Prize in 1993. On May 10, 1994, he was inaugurated South Africa's first democratically elected President. He went on to become a hero to many, a champion of the underprivileged and an icon of freedom world-wide. He passed away at his home in Johannesburg on December 5, 2013.

Many thought-provoking quotes are attributed to him and there's a lesson for all us in his quote that forms the title of this piece.

"It always seems impossible until it's done."

Chapter Thirty-five

SPEAK OF THE DEVIL

We've all had, more than likely, the experience of sitting in our office chatting to a colleague when someone whose name has been mentioned pops his/her head around the door. Here, in Ireland, when this happens, we say "speak of the devil."

Or you've met a friend for coffee and, in the course of the chat, a person who came up in the conversation suddenly phones. And you reply, speak of the devil!

These incidents can be explained away as coincidences, or happy circumstance. And they very well may be, but what if it's something else? Could it be mental telepathy?

This is described as the purported transmission of information from one person to another without using any of our known sensory channels, or physical interaction.

Note the word "purported."

It's hard to accept that the incident I'm going to describe was a coincidence. Does that mean it was mental telepathy?

Here's the story.

Back in the early 2000s, I became friendly with a safety consultant from the U.K. I can't recall how we became acquainted, but most times he had business in Dublin, we met for a coffee or a meal, and as I worked in the safety business, we shared a common interest. Daniel (not his real name) had a most interesting approach in changing staff attitudes and behaviours in the safety field. Every safety initiative that I knew about, before meeting Daniel, revolved around changing people's attitudes. This, in turn, was expected to lead to a decrease in unsafe behaviours. Nothing wrong with that – it works to a lesser or greater extent.

His approach was the opposite and it worked like this. Take, say, the top ten unsafe behaviours which led to the most accidents (not every unsafe behaviour did every time, of course). Have a work "champion" observe behaviours in the workplace for 30 minutes daily and post the results. And guess what happened over time? The number of unsafe behaviours reduced, while the attitudes of the staff to safety changed considerably, resulting in positive results all round.

He wrote a book about this concept and gifted me a signed copy which I kept in a bookcase in my office. As it happened, his trips to Dublin became fewer and fewer. Our meet-ups became less and less, till they finally ended. Then we lost touch with each other altogether.

Some years later, I was holding a safety meeting in my office when the subject of attitudes and behaviours came up in the conversations. I went to the bookcase saying I had a book about that very subject there. But there was no trace of it. Puzzled, I turned and asked the people present, had I lent it to anyone. Everyone present denied ever seeing it.

I expressed disappointment that the book had seemingly disappeared, as it had been given to me by my friend Daniel, whom I hadn't heard from in a few years and then I resumed the meeting.

The meeting later ended and the attendees returned to their desks elsewhere in the building. An hour later my desk phone rang: It was one of people at the meeting. "Apologies Ted," she said, "but I found the book here in my office – I'd forgotten all about it." I responded: "great news, I'm glad you found, as I'd hate to lose it. Drop it up to me when you're passing," and I put down the phone.

Immediately after I hung up the phone, an email flashed on my computer screen. "Hi Ted, how are you keeping? It's been a while since we've been in touch. I'm here in the USA for the last three years working in a university."

It was, you've guessed it, my long-lost friend Daniel!

I got such a shock that I jumped from my chair and ran towards the door. How could this happen? How could someone that I'd been speaking about earlier and who I hadn't seen, or spoken to, for a number of years, choose this exact time to contact me?

An amazing coincidence, or proof of mental telepathy?

I immediately responded to the email and that was it – I never heard from him again.

So, was it a coincidence, was it mental telepathy, or could it really, really, really, have been speak of the devil?

What do you think?

Chapter Thirty-six

ARE MISSION STATEMENTS EVER READ?

Nowadays, most companies or organisation, profit or not-for-profit has a mission statement. But does it clearly communicate what it is they do in concise and simple language, avoiding business jargon?

Many of the mission statements I've seen seemed more like the author(s) were attempting to win the Nobel Prize for Literature, rather than give a simple message both to their employees and clients/customers/members.

A properly crafted mission statement gives direction and focus to management and staff, while at the same time letting clients know what to expect.

Mission statements that are mostly unintelligible to employees and clients alike are a waste of space.

I can recall once reading such a statement in the reception area of a large hospital. Hung on the wall in a conspicuous place, it took me about a minute to read and probably five to understand. I said to myself wouldn't it be far simpler and clearer if it just said, "We help sick people." After all, isn't that what hospitals do the world over? No

ambiguity and easily understood. Why hide this simple message in a barrage of long words and longer sentences?

Several studies have revealed that many employees have no idea what their organisation mission statement says, never mind being inspired and motivated by it. Similar studies reveal that companies whose staff understand and are motivated by the statement do better than those that do not.

There is another angle to mission statements, however. Even when these are well crafted and easily understood, do the employees believe that the organisation actually lives up to the promise? Again, studies reveal that a high percentage of employees do not.

I can't tell you what the mission statements of the banking industry prior to the great crash in the late 2000s were but I could bet they were mostly contradicted by the banks actions and decisions at the time. How many other industries have fine statements but contradict them at every hand's turn?

Finally, here is an example from Toastmasters International that meets the criteria for a simple and inspiring Mission Statement.

"We empower individuals to become more effective communicators and leaders."

Is it time you checked your organisation's statement?

Chapter Thirty-seven

NO AWARENESS - NO CHANGE

Change is impossible without awareness, so how do we become aware? Aware of what you might ask? That's a good question and the answer depends on your particular situation. It could be personal, organisational, national, or something entirely different.

Being aware of what is happening in your organisation and understanding its strengths and weaknesses is a major advantage, if you're in a position to effect the desired change. Lacking this awareness can lead to under performance and a belief that everything in the garden is rosy. Then it happens, when without warning, you are suddenly and painfully made aware.

This is what happened to me when I attended my first Toastmasters International Convention in Las Vegas, in August 1992, as a district officer representing the U.K. and Ireland.

Blissfully unaware of our poor performance in meeting the district's KPIs, I rubbed shoulders with many leaders from Australia, New Zealand and Southern Africa. To my consternation, the Toastmasters districts in these countries were hugely successful and at the top of their game, while ours was dragging along at the bottom.

It was not a nice feeling, I can tell you. The problem was that up to then, I had no idea, and was completely unaware, of how poorly we were performing in relation to the rest of the world.

The good news is that now we knew how poorly our district was performing, we came up with a new strategy, introduced it when we got back home, and by June 1993, our district was proudly placed among the leading districts in the world and best of all far ahead of our buddies in Australia, New Zealand and Southern Africa. What quiet satisfaction!

Change always needs the creation of awareness first – otherwise things stay the same.

Chapter Thirty-eight

THE 7 HABITS OF HIGHLY SUCCESSFUL LEADERS

#1 They have a "Why." In other words, they have a strong belief and passion for what they want to achieve.

#2 They have a vision and are able to communicate it to all concerned. They don't communicate it just once, but constantly.

#3 They set SMART goals. Goals that are specific, measurable, achievable, realistic and with a time deadline.

#4 They lead as well as manage. They understand that leadership is action, not position. If management is the "What", then leadership is the "How."

#5 Their teams share high levels of trust between members.

#6 They instil in their teams a belief that they will be successful. Negativity never gets a mention.

#7 They get started!

Chapter Thirty-nine

THE LEADERSHIP BUS

I consider the book "The Leadership Bus" as the best leadership book ever written. Not surprising, I suppose, as I wrote it!

Okay, I confess to making this false and unjustifiable claim just to get your attention!

The idea came to me at a Toastmasters regional training event in a hotel in Las Vegas. I was leading a session of district leaders, due to take over the top district job a few weeks later on July 1.

I remember telling them that as they went asleep before midnight on June 30, they expected that they would wake up the next morning on July 1 as the same person. But, to everyone else in the district, they had changed overnight, because on July 1 they had become the big boss. The boss who was now the "numero uno."

I said, "your members are now looking to you for a vision, for direction, for leadership. If you don't know where you're going, nobody else will either."

Then this idea struck me and I went on to say: "you're a bit like a bus driver who has no destination in mind. In that case the bus never leaves the garage." I drew a very bad image of a bus on a flipchart and an even worse image of the driver sitting at the wheel. "This could be you on the first of July, in charge of your district, but no idea where you're going," I told them.

Leaders are expected to have a vision and to be able to communicate it to all their followers.

Now that my creative juices were flowing, I confirmed that the next step after deciding the destination (the vision), was to persuade the followers to get on the bus (the journey) with them.

When a leader sets out their vision, would-be followers usually fall into three categories. The first group can't wait to get involved (get on the bus), the second group needs some persuasion and the third group indicate very little interest, if any. Better leave these behind at all costs as they will begin to undermine the others by their negative behaviours.

Everything in place, the bus moves off towards its destination with a trusted driver at the wheel and an enthusiastic team on board. What could go wrong? Well, a lot, unless the team are treated properly. Team members may get fed up, dissatisfied, not appreciated and switch off mentally, or, in extreme cases, leave the organisation. In bus parlance they leave the bus. It's the leader's job to ensure this doesn't happen.

The training session moved on and I didn't give the bus analogy a second thought until people started telling me how they now saw their leadership journey in a different light.

Three years later, in 2008, I finally wrote the book.

Chapter Forty

IF YOU DON'T ASK, NOBODY WILL HEAR YOU

Why are so many of us reluctant to ask for help? In the old days, we men, in particular, when unsure of our location usually while driving, were quite infamous for not asking for directions. We would prefer to drive around in circles for ages, before we'd stoop to stopping and asking for directions. Male pride can be a powerful disincentive to admitting that we're lost. Nowadays, of course, with GPS, everyone knows exactly how to get from A to B, even if you hear the dreaded word "recalculating" a number of times!

In 1992, after the Toastmasters Convention in Las Vegas, I headed off to Walla Walla, Washington, to see my mother's first cousin, my second cousin. Helen and my grandmother, her aunt, were very close, exchanging letters frequently, and she even visited Ireland on one occasion to see her. I felt it only right to repay the compliment on my first visit to the USA.

Landing in Portland, Oregon, I had no idea how I was going to get from there to Walla Walla. At my hotel, I found there was a daily rail service from Portland to Chicago which stopped en route, at a small station named Pendleton, in eastern Oregon. Next morning, I presented myself at the railway station, hoping against hope that I would find a way to get from Pendleton to my destination. The ticket clerk was very helpful, even phoning the staff in Pendleton. No luck; there was no bus service to Walla Walla. The best thing, he said, is ask the conductor on the train and he may be able to help. So, off I set on a lengthy rail journey, which for a lot of the route, ran alongside the magnificent Columbia River. The conductor passed by once, or twice, but, as he seemed to be busy, I refrained from interrupting him.

Finally, I arrived in Pendleton. As I exited the carriage with my suitcase, a man was hugging his wife beside the carriage door, obviously about to depart. I went back in, collected my carry-on and as I stepped on the platform, the man boarded the train and sat in exactly the same seat I had just vacated.

I saw the conductor walking in my direction and as he drew level, I asked him: "Sir, can you tell me how I might get from here to Walla Walla?" "I'm sorry," he replied, "I can't help you, but those men at the end of the platform may do". I looked to where he was pointing and saw two men at the far end, the only other people on the entire platform. Before I could do anything, I heard this female voice behind me: "you want to go to Walla Walla?" It was the lady who had just left her husband on the train and who was now looking out the window at us. "Yes," I said, "I'm visiting my cousin who lives there." "I'm from there and I'm happy to take you back with me," she said. I couldn't believe it! What a coincidence! I was overjoyed. Such was my relief that, spontaneously, I threw my arms around her and gave her a long huge hug.

As I released her, I turned around just as the train moved off. I can still see her husband's face as he stared in disbelief out the carriage window. Can you imagine what must have been going through his mind? He had just bid a fond farewell to his wife and before the train had left the station, a stranger who had just alighted was hugging her tightly. There were no cell or mobile phones back then, so he had to wait until he reached his destination before clarifying the situation. Wouldn't you like to be a fly on the wall during that conversation?

Mrs Shannon, for that was her name, another coincidence, for Shannon is the name of the longest river in Ireland, brought me back to Walla Walla and deposited me at the front door of my cousin's home.

I had arrived safe and sound. You see, if you don't ask, nobody will hear you.

Chapter Forty-one

NONE OF US IS AS SMART AS ALL OF US

This is supposedly a Japanese proverb and there is a whole lot of truth in it.

How many times have we individually decided to do something and, after discussing it with somebody, changed our mind partially, or indeed completely?

Why are there government cabinets, boards of directors and committees, except that the more intellect that's applied to decisions, the better and stronger are the decisions made?

Of course, not every decision is, or must be, unanimous. Differences of opinion are valuable, as they can help prevent "group think" deciding the argument or debate.

However, if the powerful members of a group are leaning in a certain direction, then there is a strong possibility that the weaker members will go along with that, even if they have personal reservations.

The answer to that is appointing a devil's advocate.

A dictionary definition of a devil's advocate is:

"Someone who pretends in an argument or discussion to be against an idea or plan that a lot of people support, in order to make people discuss and consider it in more detail."

Example: I was just playing devil's advocate, so that you could consider a different point of view.

The appointment of such an advocate doesn't always appeal to leaders who can't, or won't, brook contrary ideas. But these are the very circumstances where a devil's advocate role is vital and that can add a completely new dimension to the discussion.

Many leaders need cheerleaders to back everything they say, or do, as they can suffer from insecurities. But, the really smart ones will surround themselves with people who will not be afraid to ask the really hard questions.

"I not only use all the brains I have, but all I can borrow, and I have borrowed a lot."

Woodrow Wilson, 28th US president, Nobel laureate (1856-1924).

Chapter Forty-two

WHY WHAT HOW

For a team to perform to a high standard, each member needs to understand why he/she is doing it, what exactly is their role, and possess the necessary skills and know-how to get it done.

First the "Why."

If employees do not know the importance of the jobs they're doing, how can they be expected to perform at a high level. They need to know the benefit to the organisation for performing well and the downside for doing it badly. It goes without saying that employees must also be aware of the effect these outcomes will have on themselves, for good, or for ill. It's always management's job to ensure that the "why" is clearly understood. How the employee's role impacts on the mission of the organisation and how this relates to the work of other departments is the minimum required.

Next the "What."

You may think that every employee knows the job he/she is expected to do, but this may not always be the case. If the job is not described in detail, then the employees must guess a lot, often doing things that they

shouldn't be involved in. Are expectations made clear like emails must be replied to with 24 hours, or when a problem requiring higher up attention is referred, or the deadline for the submission of a report made clear?

It's very clear that a detailed job description is the basic requirement. A job description which is discussed with the employee and then given to him/her. A job description that is specific but yet cannot be interpreted as a reason to be micro managed.

Finally, the "How."

Let's assume you're a junior manager and expected to be able to motivate your staff. But, has anyone ever shown you how to do this, or sent you on a course to learn this skill?

Or take another situation. One of your employees comes to you and asks you to show them how to do something. And your answer is along the lines of, "If I have to tell you how to do everything, why are you working here."

Some of the main reasons why employees don't know how to do tasks they are supposed to do are:

1. It's assumed they know how to do it.
2. Training isn't up to an acceptable standard.
3. The time to train employees properly can't be spared. Everyone is too busy.

If you really want to know if your employees are capable of doing something, don't ask them can they do it; rather ask them to show you.

Chapter Forty-three

MONEY WON'T MAKE YOU HAPPY, BUT HAPPY PEOPLE WILL MAKE YOU MONEY

This quote is attributed to the Financial Times of London. But is it the case?

Whatever about money not making you happy (in my opinion, a certain amount will cause you to be less sad, at least!), happy, satisfied employees go a long way to making a well-run company more successful.

Why should this be the case?

Several studies have revealed that extra money doesn't make employees as happy, as feeling they're making a positive contribution that is seen and acknowledged.

In this positive state, call it happy if you like, they keep an open mind, listen to other peoples' opinions, accept constructive feedback and get on well with their peers and colleagues.

One study concluded that the greatest predictor of a team's achievements was how they felt about each other. It's also the case that one bad apple can damage that sense of togetherness. In my book "The Leadership Bus" I write about ensuring that these bad apples are not permitted on the bus. Just as one bad apple in a barrel will over time rot the whole lot, a negative, angry, member of a team will cause it to under-perform.

In Richard Conniff's book: "The Ape in the Corner Office: How to Make Friends, Win Fights, and Work Smarter by Understanding Human Nature," it turns out that the fifteen high-performance teams he studied, averaged 5.6 positive interactions for every negative one. On the other hand, the nineteen low-performance teams racked up a positive/negative ratio of just .363. That is, they had about three negative interactions for every positive one.

Just to be clear, these are interactions with other team members.

Something to think about, isn't it?

Chapter Forty-four

"I HAVE A DREAM"

When I was in Washington, D.C., for the first time, in late August 2006, attending the Toastmasters International Annual Convention, one of the highlights was visiting the Lincoln Memorial. I was intent on standing on the exact spot where Dr. Martin Luther King delivered his iconic inspirational speech on August 28, 1963 to a crowd estimated to be near 250,000 people.

Having previously seen only photos of the Memorial, I was unprepared for its size and grandeur. Making my way on foot from the Washington Monument, I first came upon the Lincoln Memorial Reflecting Pool. As I progressed alongside this, the Memorial area grew ever larger, until it loomed before me with what seemed like hundreds of steps leading to the summit.

Consisting of 164 acres in total, it was opened on May 30, 1922, in honour of Abraham Lincoln, the 16th President of the United States.

After visiting the impressive central chamber, housing the towering statue of Lincoln, I began to look around for information regarding the exact location where Dr. King delivered his famous speech. It took me a while to find it, hidden around a corner of another chamber. Certainly, not easy to find. Following the instructions, I exited the main portal, turned to my left and there a few steps down was the pretty faded, identifying, inscription engraved on the flat well-worn stone.

I stood there and gazed over the Memorial Pool towards the Washington Monument, with the Dome on Capitol Hill visible in the distance and reflected on that special day in 1963.

I began to think of the issues that brought so many people to this gathering, many travelling great distances. I thought of the emotional atmosphere that existed at this place and time, generated largely by the inspirational words of Dr. King. I imagined what it must have been like to have been there, standing shoulder to shoulder in the blistering heat, listening to the beliefs, dreams, and overdue freedoms of your people being articulated so passionately and so powerfully. As I stood there, 43 years later almost to the day, I also reflected on the changes inspirational speeches have made in the world – speeches that are remembered long after the event; too many to mention here but we all have our favourites.

The word inspire comes from Latin. The Oxford Dictionary defines it as "filling (someone) with the urge or ability to do or feel something, especially to do something creative.

His philosophy inspired a later generation of environmentalists"

An inspirational speech differs greatly from a persuasive one in that an inspirational speech touches a person's emotions (the heart), while a persuasive speech relates to a person's rational senses (the head). You will always recognise an inspirational speech when you hear one, as you will feel it emotionally.

Read the last few lines of Dr. King's speech below, and I guarantee you that despite being removed in place, time, and distance from August 28, 1963 you will still feel emotionally affected.

> *"And so, let freedom ring from the prodigious hilltops of New Hampshire.*
> *Let freedom ring from the mighty mountains of New York.*
> *Let freedom ring from the heightening Alleghenies of Pennsylvania!*
> *Let freedom ring from the snow-capped Rockies of Colorado.*
> *Let freedom ring from the curvaceous peaks of California. But not only that.*
> *Let freedom ring from Stone Mountain of Georgia.*
> *Let freedom ring from Lookout Mountain of Tennessee.*
> *Let freedom ring from every hill and every molehill of Mississippi, from every mountainside, let freedom ring!*
> *And when this happens, when we allow freedom to ring, when we let it ring from every village and every hamlet, from every state and every city, we will be able to speed up that day when all of God's children, black men and white men,*

Jews and Gentiles, Protestants and Catholics, will be able to join hands and sing in the words of the old Negro spiritual: "Free at last! Free at last! Thank God Almighty, we are free at last!"

A wish, I'm sure, that could be re-echoed by very many people in several countries throughout the world, even today.

Chapter Forty-five

DO YOU KNOW ANY GRASSHOPPERS?

If you're from the west of Ireland, and lived in the countryside there, you will most likely know what a grasshopper is. Where I came from, these insects, near relatives of crickets, were very common during the summer months in rough grassland and boggy ground, but I believe their numbers have declined since, as their habitat has reduced due to more intensive farming. You always heard them before you saw them, as they made a particular sound caused by the insect rubbing its long hind legs against its forewings, known as stridulation. Not many of us knew that!

They are strong flyers and many a time as I came close to them, especially on warm sunny days, when they are most active, they would make a short flight to a new spot just a few metres away, where they would remain silent for a while before recommencing their songs.

Hatching in May, by June, they are fully grown and mature. They then enjoy a wonderful summer of singing, dancing, and courting, with no thought to what is about to happen to them when the first frosts arrive. You've guessed it – they then keel over and die!

Do you know any human equivalent of a grasshopper? Someone who flits around month after month, year after year, having a wonderful time, but not advancing their careers one bit. They move from job to job, never settling on any particular one. They begin many courses, but never finish any of them. They travel the world, moving from one country to another, but never putting down roots.

Then, suddenly, reality bites. In their '30s, they begin to think of settling down with a spouse, or partner, and starting a family, but a decade or more has been lost, resulting in possible negative effects which I don't have to spell out here.

A young son of a friend of mine quit college after a year, moved out of home to a nearby city and began a job working in a supermarket. Month followed month, the city life was very appealing, and good times were being had. After a year, or so, later, he happened to be in Dublin and I invited him to lunch. Eventually, the conversation got around to his future and what he intended to do with his life. I told him he reminded me of a grasshopper, telling him, as I've related earlier, that there is only so much singing, dancing, and courting one can do, before the first frosts of the winter undo the unwary.

He must have taken my motivational speech (!) to heart, as he went back to college, trained as an apprentice and ended up in a well-paid and secure job. He is now happily married with four young children.

Whenever we have met up since, I still good naturedly refer him as the grasshopper who survived!

Maybe there is a "grasshopper" you know who could avoid an approaching "winter frost", if you told them the story?

Chapter Forty-six

WALKING MY FIELDS

Back in the '80s, as previously related, I was the Station Master at Heuston Railway Station, Dublin. It consisted of the concourse, platforms and offices, like any other station. But, in addition, the entire area, which extended over at least 100 acres, included a maintenance depot, a freight depot, and a train signalling centre (known in the local jargon as the signal cabin), a parcels office and a large car park.

My office was located off platform 2, convenient to the comings and goings of trains and people, which went on all the time.

Two or three times a week, I used to leave my office in the early afternoon and visit all these locations, speaking and listening to the staff and observing the activities.

Before I had ever heard of the term, I had unwittingly discovered "Management by Walking Around," or MBWA. This became a business management term in the '70s, but it hadn't arrived in Ireland yet!

It's a wonderful way of keeping in touch with staff members, listening to their ideas and concerns, updating them on current business issues, while observing the tasks they are performing.

Then I made a discovery. The days I stayed in the office for these hours, I received several queries/requests, but on the days I did my walkabout, on arriving back in my office, my secretary would have only one or two calls for me to return.

How was this? The answer was staring me in the face. When I was in the office in the afternoons, I got deluged with calls: but in the hours I was doing my MBWA thing, the callers, due to my non-availability, found other solutions to their problems.

The obvious lesson is the more accessible you are, the more calls you'll get – callers that could and should have found answers elsewhere, if they only made the attempt. It's not as easy nowadays to avoid these types of calls with the arrival of smart phones, unless they're turned off or, come to think of it, put in aircraft mode!

Then I had a visit from a journalist from a Dublin evening newspaper who wished to write an article about me and the role of the Station Master. During our conversation, I mentioned my visits to my other bases and in an attempt to find words to describe this behaviour, I reverted to my country roots. Every farmer nearby where I came from, worthy of the name, would walk around his farm each day to inspect his crops, animals and fences. It was known as walking the fields.

Lo and behold, when the nearly full-page article finally appeared, the headline splashed across the top read:

"Walking the Fields of Heuston Station" with a photo of me alongside.

So, overnight, a new description for MBWA was born and for country people at heart, like me, it's a lot more powerful. Yay!

Chapter Forty-seven

SOMETIMES THE FORCE IS NOT WITH YOU

We've all had the experience of looking forward for ages to meeting somebody, going somewhere, visiting a place you always wanted to visit, and at the last very last minute, ending up disappointed.

The closer you came to the longed-for event, the more disappointing it became to have it snatched from you, in front of your nose, as it were.

This is what happened to me on my visit to Colorado/Wyoming in May 2008, on Toastmasters business.

My friends Dana and John ferried me from Denver to, first, Rapid City in South Dakota. Then back to Wyoming to the city of Gillette where a high percentage of the coal production in the USA is mined. Then to the Mount Rushmore National Memorial to view a massive sculpture carved into Mount Rushmore in the Black Hills region of South Dakota. The 60ft high granite faces depict U.S. Presidents George Washington, Thomas Jefferson, Theodore Roosevelt and Abraham Lincoln. This sculpture is, indeed, an awe-inspiring sight which took 14 years of endeavour, before being finally completed in 1941.

Next up was the Devils Tower in northeastern Wyoming

It rises dramatically 1,267 feet (386m) above the Belle Fourche River. The summit is 5,112 feet (1,559 m) above sea level. Of course, I insisted in walking around it, while my friends waited patiently.

Devils Tower was the first declared a U.S. National Monument established on September 24, 1906, by President Theodore Roosevelt.

On the road again, we passed through a small town called Ten Sleep which is a town in Washakie County, Wyoming, United States. It is located in the Big Horn Basin in the western foothills of the Big Horn Mountains. Named Ten Sleep by the Indian nation who lived in that area because it was ten sleeps (days travel) from other places they regularly visited.

Finally, arriving in Cody, named after the famous Buffalo Bill, one of my childhood heroes that I used read about in comics and books, we rested overnight for the planned visit next day to Yellowstone National Park, the place that was top of my to-visit list. Finally, it was about to happen, or so I thought.

Yellowstone National Park is located in the states of Wyoming, Montana, and Idaho. It was established by the U.S. Congress and signed into law by President Ulysses S. Grant on March 1, 1872. Yellowstone was the first national park in the USA and is also widely regarded as being the first national park in the world.

Being just short of 100 miles from Cody to Old Faithful, it's a journey of between 2 and 3 hours depending on traffic and the season. We set off early full of hope that we would see the Park in all its grandeur and that I would see Old Faithfull, the geyser recognised far and wide as the iconic symbol of Yellowstone, in all its glory.

Alas, alas, it was not to be. We were about two thirds of the way there, when it began to snow, first lightly, then quite heavily. By the time we arrived at the Old Faithfull Lodge, we could just about see our hands in front of our faces. Staring out from the lodge to the geyser less than 100 yards away, it was totally impossible to distinguish the steam and water from the geyser and the falling blanket of snow. These eruptions occur every 90 minutes to 2 hours and last for about 2 minutes, so we had one chance and only one chance, as we had to get back on the road to Cody as quickly as we could.

Well, the chance came and went and all I could see was a white curtain of snow and steam, each quite indistinguishable one from the other.

So homewards we went, plodding our weary way like the ploughman in Wordsworth's poem, "Elegy in a Country Churchyard," stuck behind a very slow-moving snow plough all the way to Cody.

Sometimes, the force is truly not with you, so just grin and bear it, or, in modern parlance, just suck it up.

Chapter Forty-eight

OLD MAN RIVER

As someone who grew up in rural Ireland before the advent of electricity and without access to radio (TV was still a pipe dream), I was totally reliant on books for information about the outside world. Luckily, I had no shortage of these, due to the Andrew Carnegie Library service to my school and regular parcels of books all the way from Sydney, Australia, from my mother's cousin.

Some of my all-time favourites were: "The Adventures of Tom Sawyer," "The Adventures of Huckleberry Finn," and "Life on the Mississippi," all novels by the great American author Mark Twain published between 1873 and 1876.

"The Adventures of *Tom Sawyer*" is an 1876 *novel* about a young boy growing up along the Mississippi River. It is set in the 1840s in the fictional town of St. Petersburg, inspired by Hannibal, Missouri, where Twain lived as a boy. Huckleberry "Huck" Finn is a fictional character created by Twain who first appeared in this book, where he is the protagonist and narrator of its sequel.

Why did these books appeal to me so much? I suppose it was because Huck and Tom were simple country boys, aged in their early teens, who got involved in adventure after adventure, located on, or near, the great Mississippi river.

Many of the characters in the books bore somewhat uncanny resemblance to locals I knew where I lived: In Kerry, these were known as "characters." Just imagine the innocence of the following exchange:

"It's lovely to live on a raft. We had the sky, up there, all speckled with stars, and we used to lay on our backs and look up at them, and discuss about whether they was made, or only just happened- Jim he allowed they was made, but I allowed they happened; I judged it would have took too long to make so many."

As I also lived about half a mile from the nearest small river, where I fished and swam in the summer, I could only imagine a river as long and as wide as the Mississippi, deep enough for steam boats and barges to navigate.

And then, many years later, I was in New Orleans after attending my cousin's wedding in nearby Baton Rouge. I wandered alone down a street and saw the tramline before me. Being at heart, a railway man, I naturally went to explore further. Arriving at the line, I saw a high grassy embankment on its far side. Curious to see what was on the other side, I climbed up and there before me in all its magnificent grandeur was the Mississippi of my childhood.

Guess what I did next? I made my way to the edge, put my hand in the water and said, "hello Mississippi, so nice to meet you after all these years."

Nearly forty years after seeing it in my child's imagination, I had at last met and greeted Old Man River. And, believe me, it was quite a sentimental experience.

Chapter Forty-nine

YOU WILL BE THE SAME PERSON IN FIVE YEARS...

"You will be the same person in five years as you are today except for the people you meet and the books you read," are the words of Charlie "Tremendous" Jones, a famous inspirational speaker in the USA, who lived from 1927 to 2008.

I can add to that the effect of the places you visit.

As I come to write the last article in this book, and reflect on Charlie's words, I can safely say that visiting places, reading books, and meeting people has changed me. When I reflect on the opportunities I've had of travelling world-wide, broadening my experiences of new languages, new cultures and new people I feel that I was specially blessed to join the Fingal Toastmasters Club in Dublin in 1985.

As I rose through the ranks in club, district, and international leadership, I made my first flight, my first trip to North America and my first visit to Asia, Australia and the Middle East. I visited the great cities of the world, saw some of its great wonders like the Grand Canyon, Niagara

Falls and the Taj Mahal, while mixing with many and varied nationalities and cultures.

I've always been an avid book reader, but visiting different countries and interacting with different people, gives you a completely different outlook on the great wide world, which you'll never get from sitting at home watching TV.

When you consider, aged 16, I made my first trip on a train, visited Dublin for the first time, and, aged 18, made my first phone call, it's amazing how the lives of teenagers have changed over the last sixty years. Now they have the world, and everything in it, at the tips of their fingers.

The question is, when they're my age, what will the teenagers then regard as normal?

Chapter Fifty

THERE HAD TO BE A CHAPTER 50!

As someone who regards himself as a reasonably balanced person(?), how could I possibly end this book with 49 chapters?

When my daughter and son-in-law pointed out that 49 was an unlucky number, I protested that I'd never heard of such a claim. Anyway, 13 has always been regarded as the unlucky number, even to the extent that some hotels avoid mentioning 13th floors. Very quickly, they smilingly pointed out that when 4 and 9 are added, the answer is 13!

So here goes with chapter 50.

As I reflect on the preceding chapters, these are the life lessons that stand out for me.

I find the words of Rabindranath Tagore (1861-1941) an Indian poet, novelist and Nobel Laureate for Literature (1913) very apt (Chapter 11). I consider his quote, "I've spent my days stringing and unstringing my instrument, while the songs I came to sing remain unsung", a wonderful metaphor for unfulfilled dreams and unrealised potential.

Why do some people never reach their full potential? Never realise their dreams?

Is it because they are short of self-belief, quit too easily or, as mentioned in Chapter 2, haven't a "Why"? No "Why" – no happy ending.

Chapter 5 reminds us of the importance of keeping the main thing the main thing – in other words sticking to our priorities. Not easy to do, but vital for success

Chapter 15 refers to Nelson Bunker Hunt's secrets of success:

"First you must decide what it is you want to achieve, then decide you're willing to pay the price to achieve it and finally pay the price."

The final piece of his advice is beyond doubt the most difficult for all of us: finishing this book is but one personal example.

The wonderful motto of my late friend, Charlie Keane, (Chapter19), "I'm not done yet" is a perfect reminder that it's never too late to stop stringing and unstringing our instruments and, finally, begin to sing our songs.

We're definitely not done yet, but this little book of life lessons definitely is!

Thank you for reading it. I hope you enjoyed it.

Ted Corcoran

ABOUT THE AUTHOR

Ted Corcoran grew up in the County Kerry countryside in Ireland. He became engrained in the culture of the area, where most communication was face to face, long before social media was even envisaged. Stories and storytellers were commonplace. Ted can recall as a small child sitting on his grandfather's knee in front of an open fire, while his grandfather regaled locals with tales of long ago.

It's no surprise then that Ted rose to prominence in Toastmasters International - the world's leading organisation in communication and leadership training. Serving as International President in 2003/2004, Ted was the first Irishman and European to do so since the organisation was founded in 1924.

ACKNOWLEDGEMENTS

This book happened when my daughter, Claire, and her husband, Ken Jackson, tired of hearing my stories, suggested I write about them. This idea came back to haunt them both, as they were later asked to assist with the editing. In the background, my wife Celine kept the home fires burning, as I turned to my creative side! Thanks Celine, Claire and Ken for your constant support and encouragement.

My good friend Gary Schmidt, past International President, Toastmasters International, volunteered his editing skills as soon as he heard I was writing the book and has encouraged me all the way. Thanks Gary.

I thank my older daughter, Sinéad, my brother Séan, and sister Mary, and their spouses and families for always being there for me through thick and thin. Familial support is so vital and so appreciated.

Finally, I thank my friend Betty Liedtke for introducing me to my publisher, Ann Aubitz, who has played a major part in shepherding me through the nuances of book publishing, while keeping her cool and moving the project ahead. Thanks Betty and Ann.